Sound at Sight

Drum Kit

book 2
Grades 5–8

by Malcolm Ball, George Double & Lorne Pearcey

Published by
Trinity College London Press Ltd
trinitycollege.com

Registered in England
Company no. 09726123

Copyright © 2010 Trinity College London
Sixth impression, March 2025

Unauthorised photocopying is illegal
No part of this publication may be copied or reproduced in any
form or by any means without the prior permission of the publisher.

Printed in England by Halstan & Co, Amersham, Bucks

Drum kit notation key

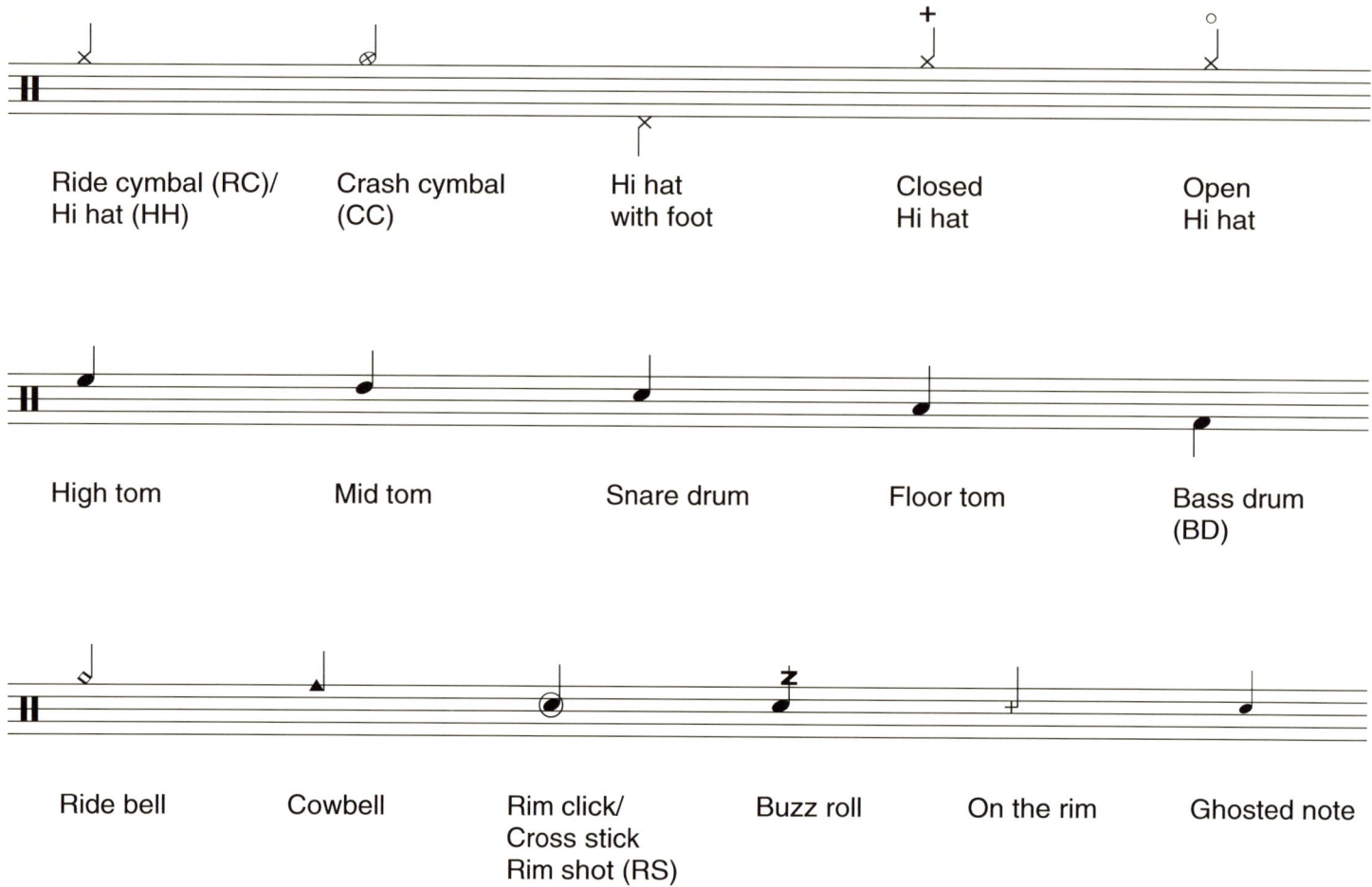

Grade 5

A wider range of styles are introduced at this grade, along with drags.

1 Reggae-ish

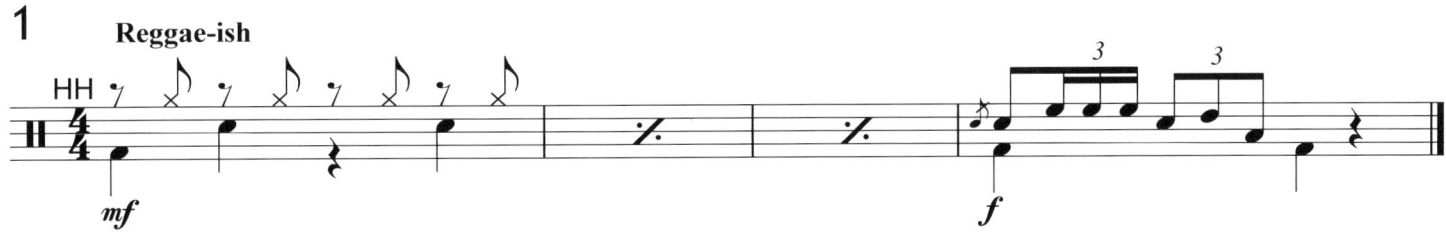

2 Swing

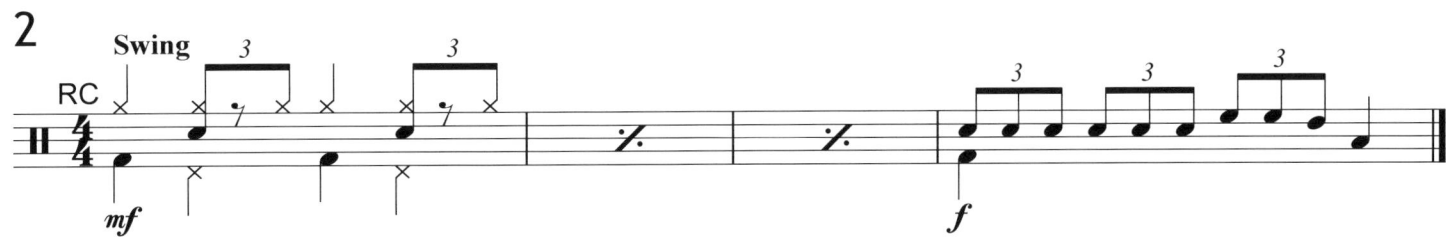

3 Funk

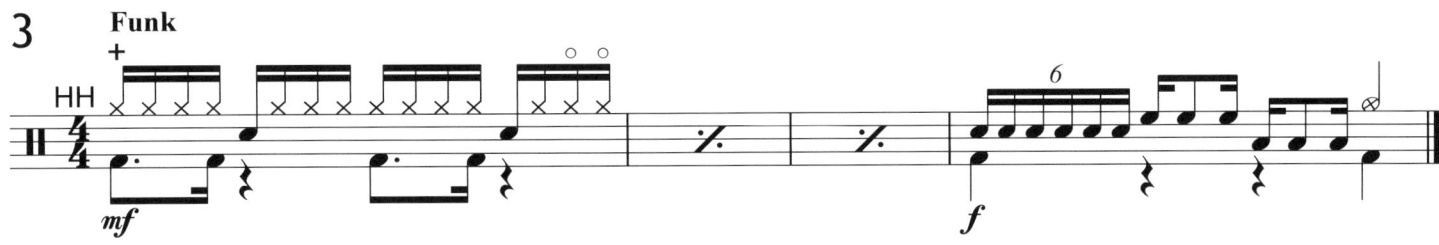

4 Steady March

Sound at Sight Drum Kit Grade 5

5 Steady groove

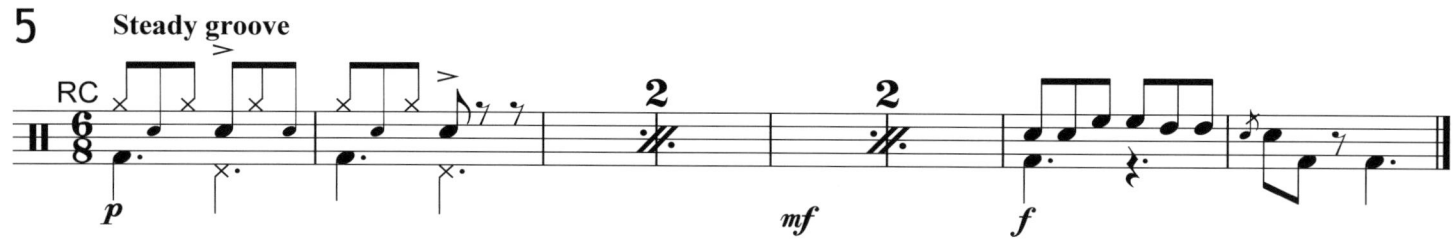

6 Swing

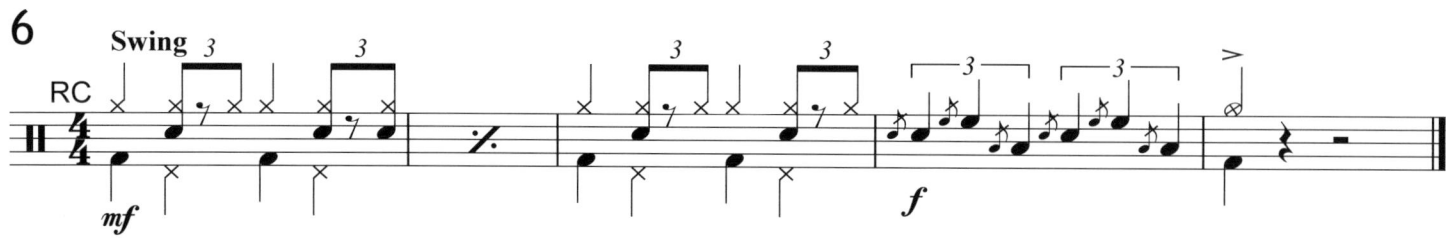

7 Latin

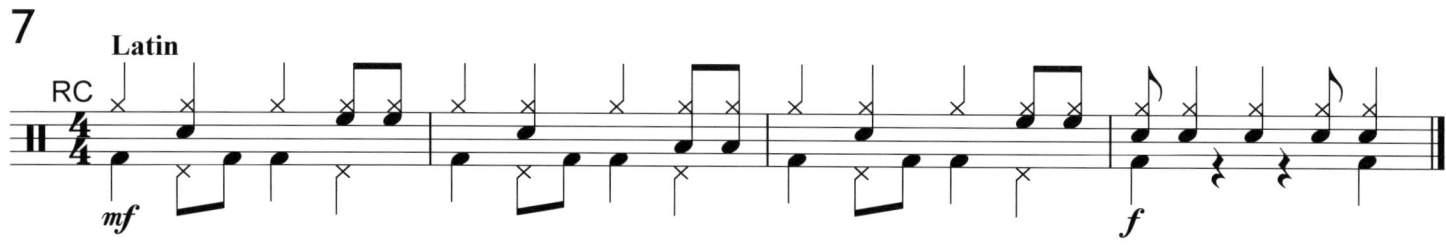

8 Indie Rock

9 Jungle

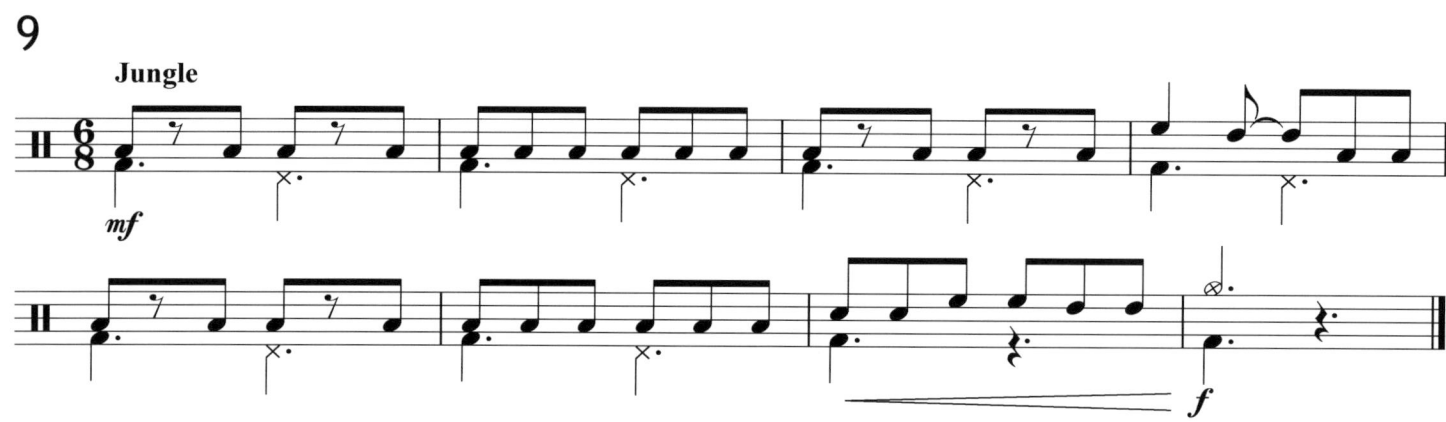

Sound at Sight Drum Kit Grade 5

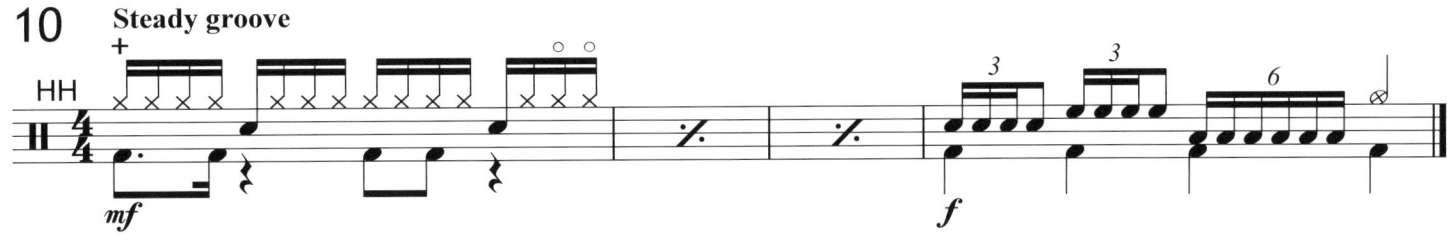

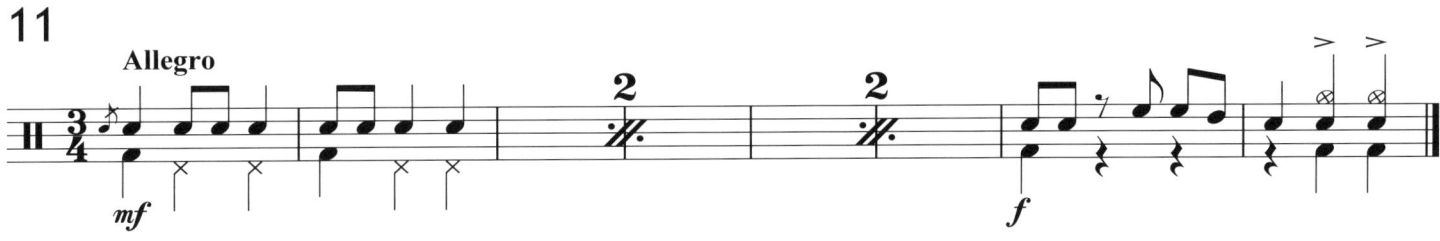

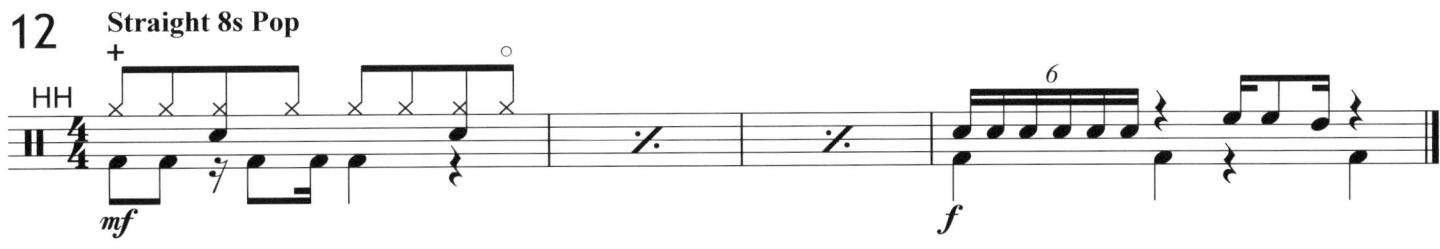

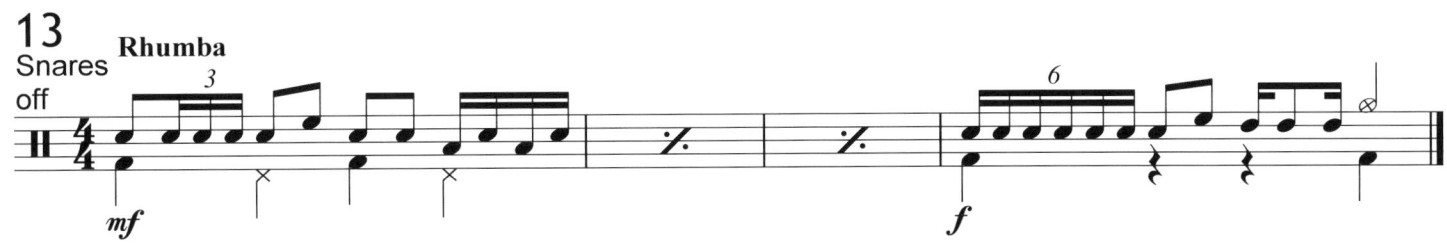

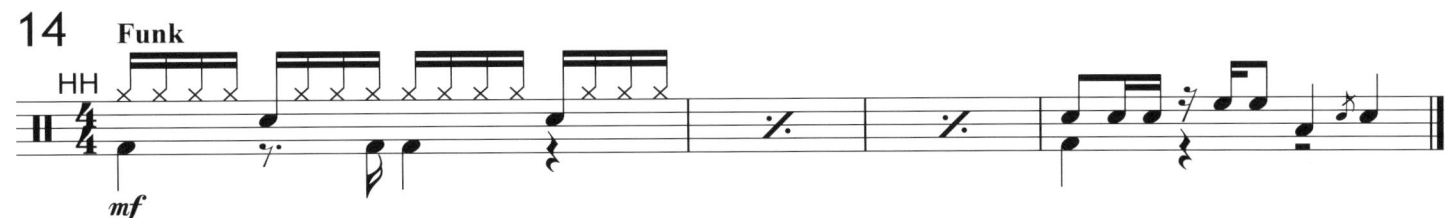

Sound at Sight Drum Kit Grade 5

Grade 6

At Grade 6, $\frac{5}{4}$ and $\frac{9}{8}$ time signatures are introduced.

Sound at Sight Drum Kit Grade 6

6 Allegro

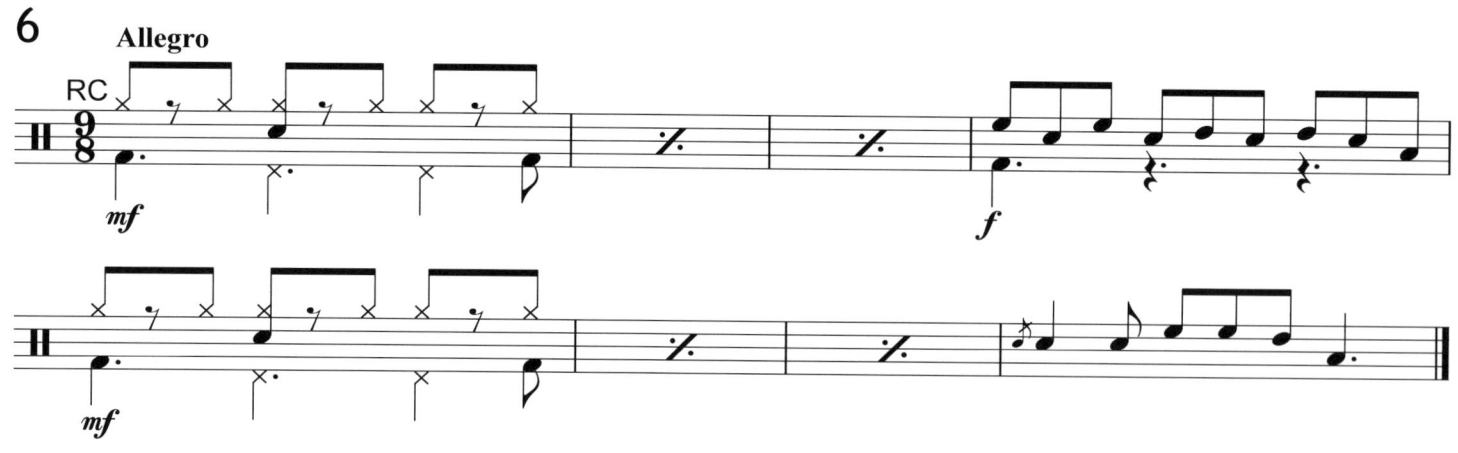

7 Bright Show 2 feel

8 Moderato

9 Tight groove

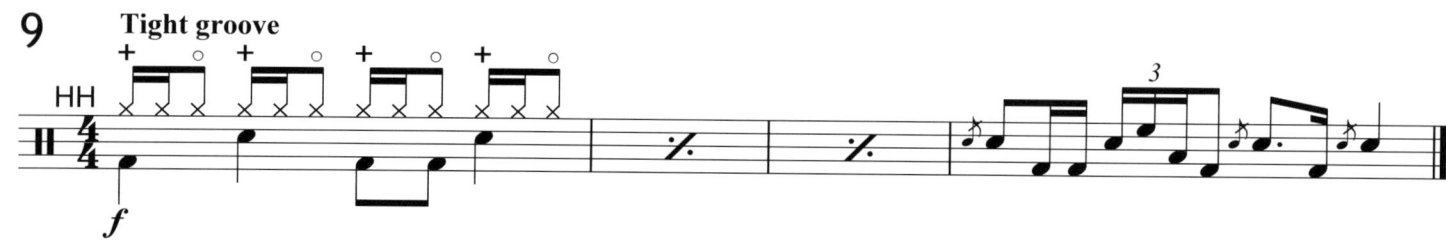

Sound at Sight Drum Kit Grade 6

Sound at Sight Drum Kit Grade 7

• Grade 7

$\frac{7}{8}$ features at this Grade.

1 **Mid-Tempo groove**

2 **Motown, with intent!**

3 **Solid Rock groove**

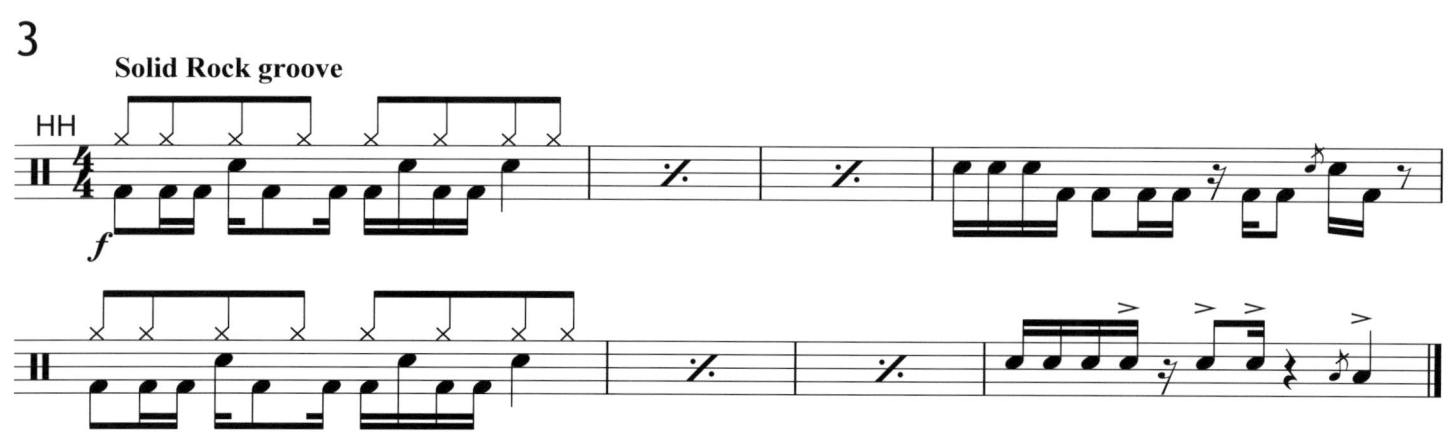

Sound at Sight Drum Kit Grade 7

Sound at Sight Drum Kit Grade 7

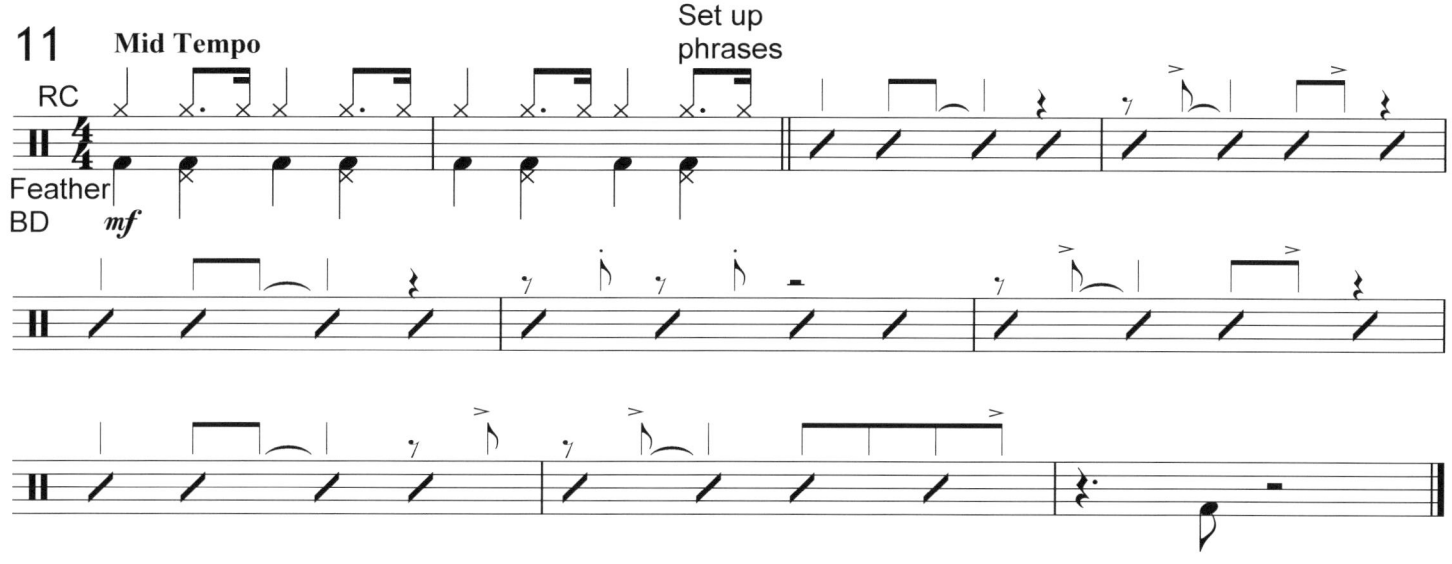

Sound at Sight Drum Kit Grade 8

• Grade 8

Grade 8 examples incorporate the parameters for all previous Grades.

1
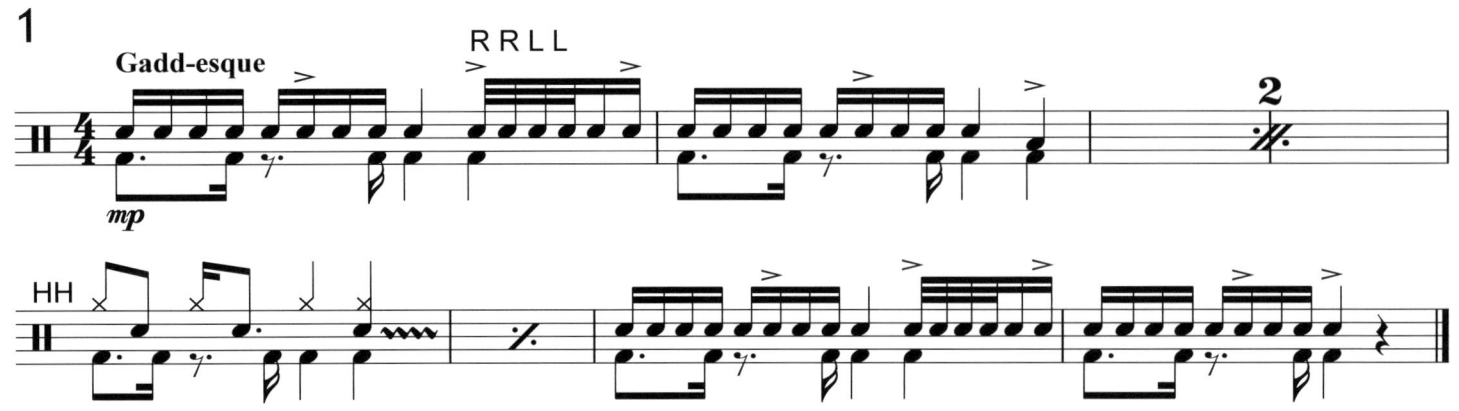

2
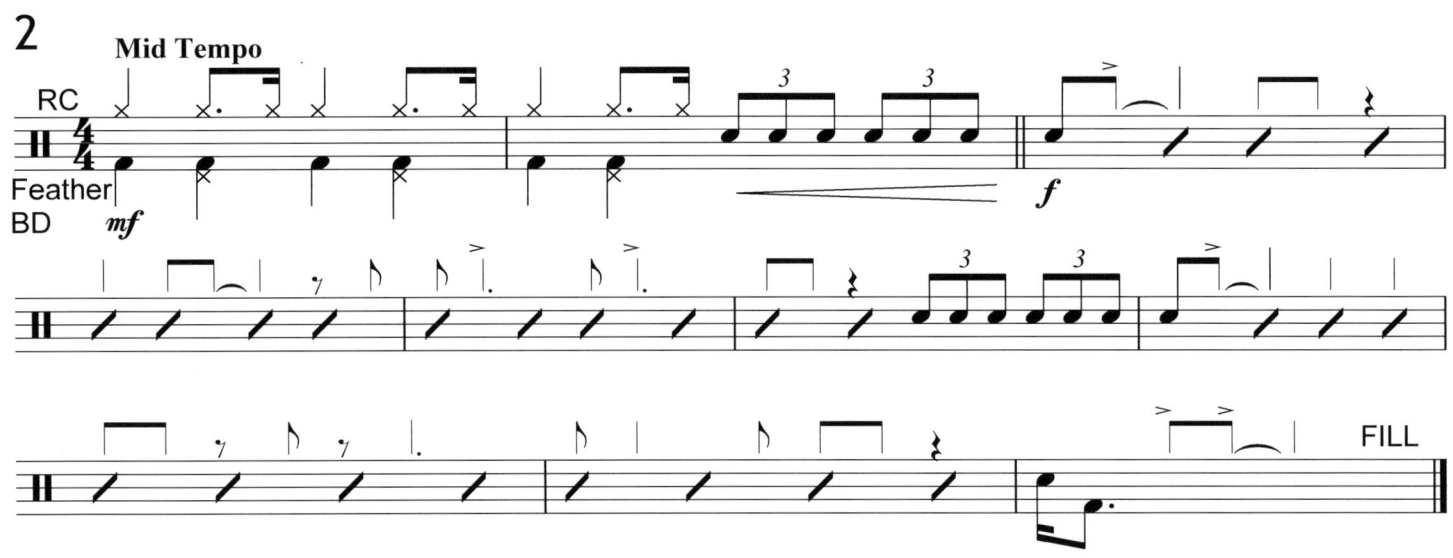

Sound at Sight Drum Kit Grade 8

3 Shuffle

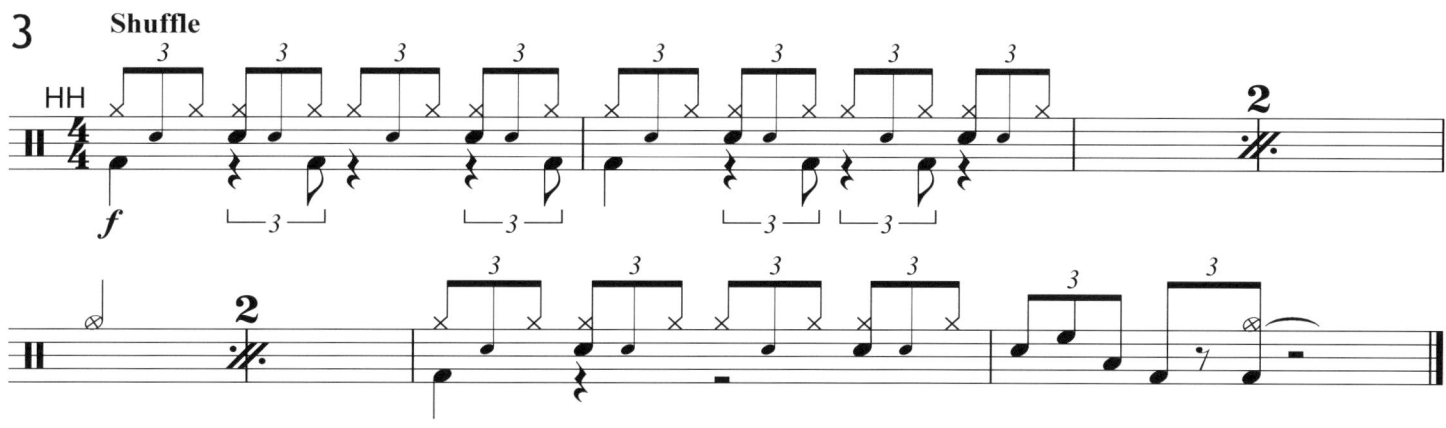

4 Half-time Shuffle

Sound at Sight Drum Kit Grade 8

5 Heavy

6 Mid Tempo groove

Sound at Sight Drum Kit Grade 8

7

8

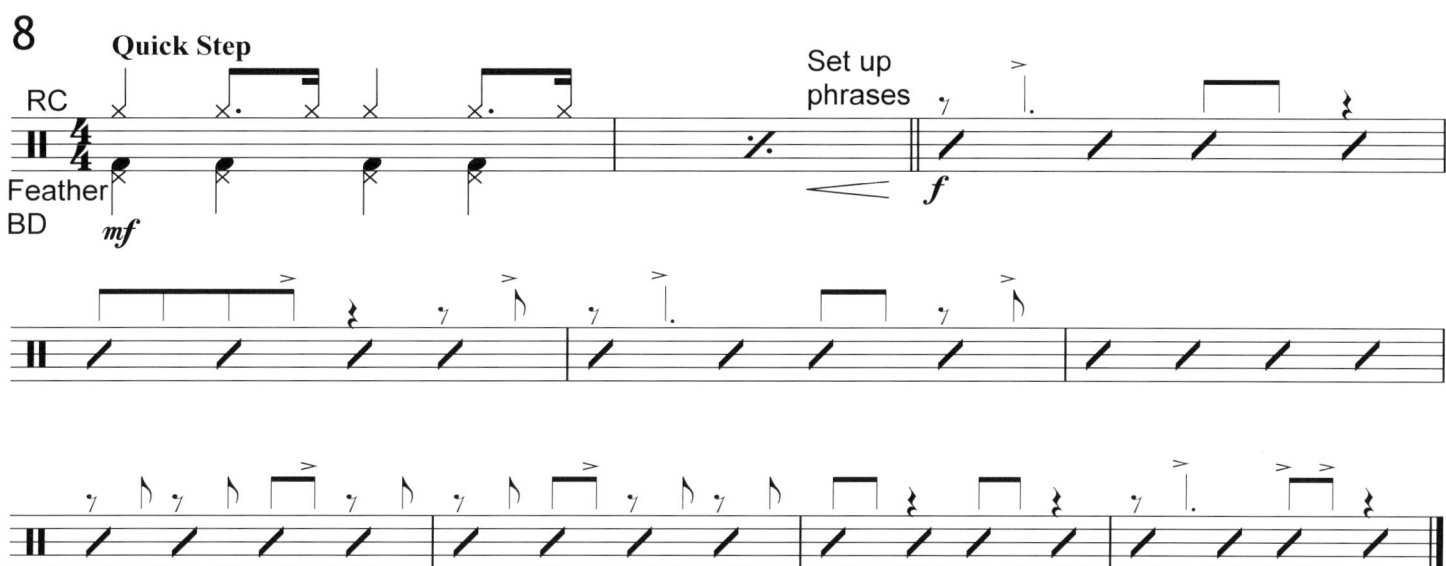

Sound at Sight Drum Kit Grade 8

9 Afro Cuban

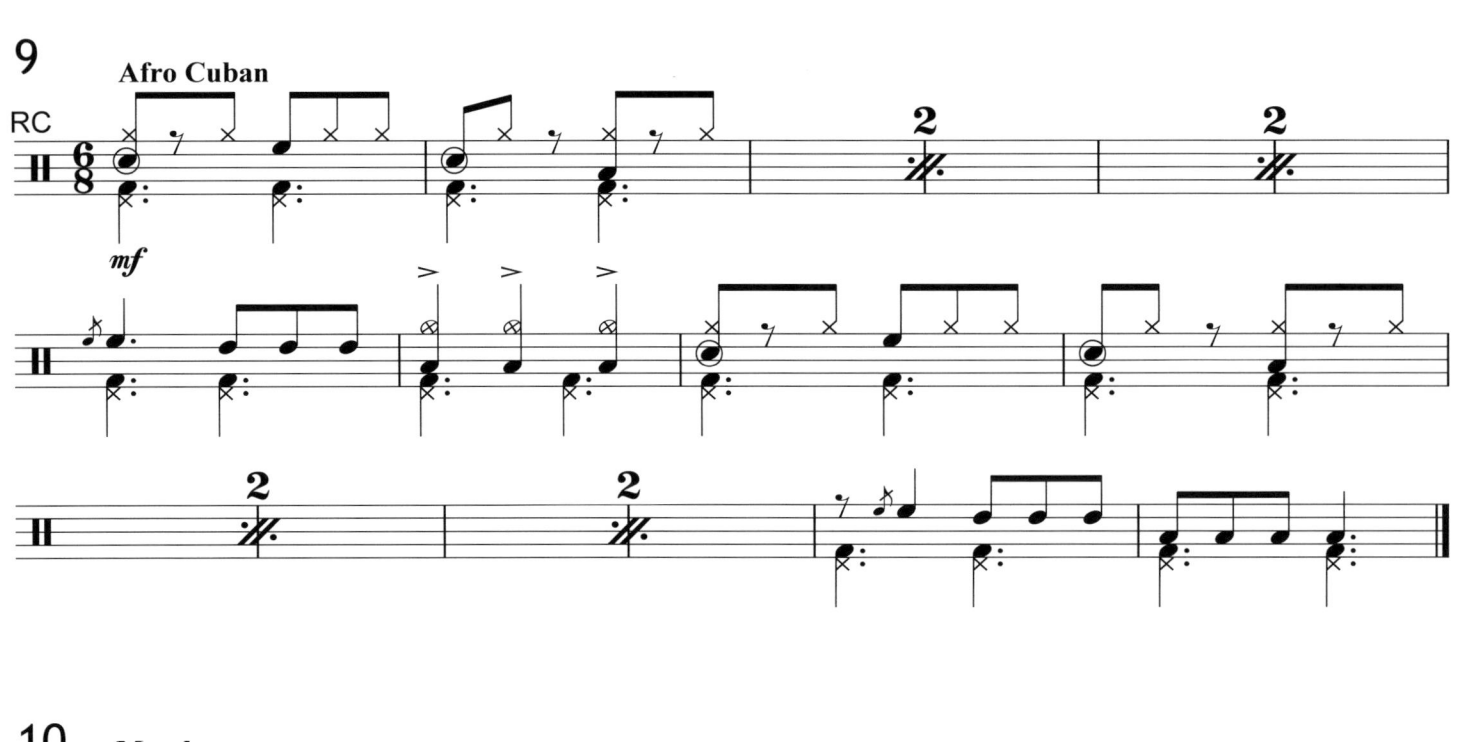

10 Mambo

Sound at Sight Drum Kit Grade 8

11 Jazz Waltz

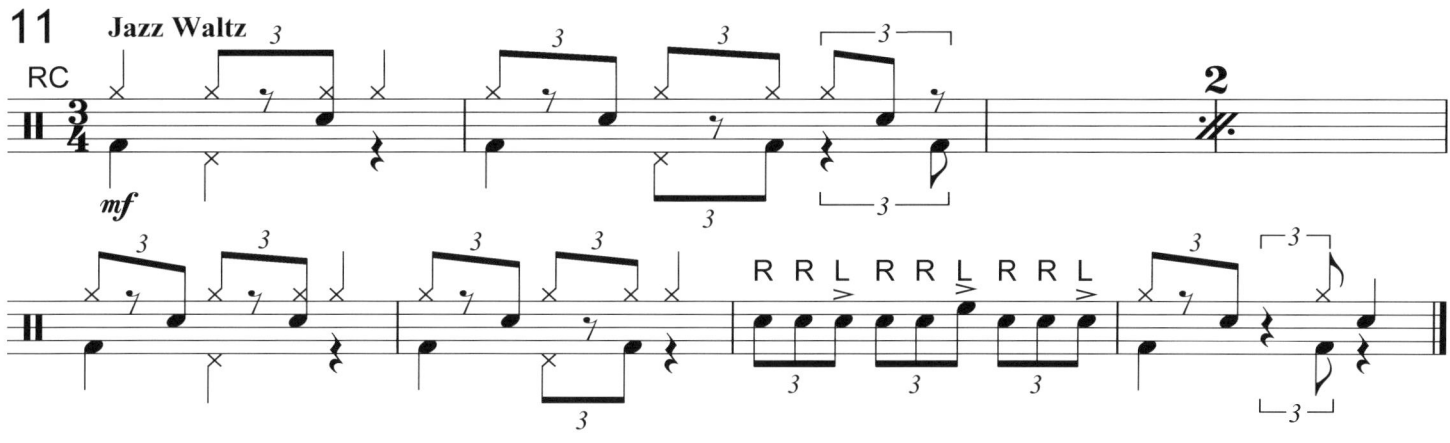

12 Funky